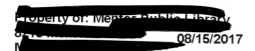

ANCIENT EARTH JOURNAL

THE LATE JURASSIC:

VOLUME 1

NOTES, DRAWINGS, AND OBSERVATIONS FROM PREHISTORY

BY JUAN CARLOS ALONSO & GREGORY S. PAUL

*For Betty and Dalí, your undying
support and endless inspiration make
everything worthwhile.
Love, Juan Carlos.*

This library edition published in 2017 by Walter Foster Jr.,
an imprint of The Quarto Group
6 Orchard Road, Suite 100
Lake Forest, CA 92630

Distributed in the United States and Canada by
Lerner Publisher Services
241 First Avenue North
Minneapolis, MN 55401 U.S.A.
www.lernerbooks.com

First Library Edition

Library of Congress Cataloging-in-Publication Data

Names: Alonso, Juan Carlos (Graphic designer), author, illustrator. | Paul, Gregory S., author.
Title: The late Jurassic : notes, drawings, and observations from prehistory
 / by Juan Carlos Alonso & Gregory S. Paul.
Other titles: Ancient Earth journal.
Description: First library edition. | Lake Forest, CA : Walter Foster Jr., an
 imprint of Quarto Publishing Group USA Inc., 2017. | Series: Ancient Earth
 journal | Audience: Ages 8+. | Includes bibliographical references and index.
Identifiers: LCCN 2017011686 | ISBN 9781942875321 (volume 1 : hardcover : alk.
 paper) | ISBN 9781942875338 (volume 2 : hardcover : alk. paper)
Subjects: LCSH: Paleontology--Jurassic--Juvenile literature. |
 Dinosaurs--Juvenile literature. | Animals, Fossil--Juvenile literature. |
 CYAC: Prehistoric animals.
Classification: LCC QE733 .A46 2017 | DDC 560.1766--dc23
LC record available at https://lccn.loc.gov/2017011686

Printed in USA
9 8 7 6 5 4 3 2 1

Table of Contents

Foreword

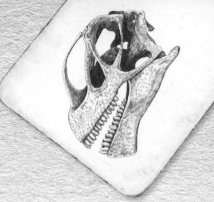

Matthew T. Mossbrucker

Director & Chief Curator

Morrison Natural History Museum, Morrison, Colorado

Jurassic! For kids (and some adults), this word immediately brings to mind images of giant dinosaurs crashing and smashing their way through a dim, primeval forest while a volcano explodes somewhere in the distance. When I was a kid reading dinosaur books like this one, I was surprised to learn that the Jurassic wasn't a where like that imaginary forest, but a when.

The word "Jurassic" refers to a special time in the history of our planet, beginning 201 million years ago and ending about 145 million years ago. Our planet is old—really, really old. The Earth is so old that we use words to tell time instead of clocks. Giving names to periods from Earth's history helps us chart time, similar to how a calendar helps us talk about when events happened in the past. "When were you born?" my kids ask me, and I say "May of 1979." When we talk about dinosaurs, they ask "When did Stegosaurus live?" and I say "The Jurassic."

The Jurassic lasted for so long that it is broken up into smaller pieces, kind of like a year is broken down into months. The Jurassic is first divided into three big chunks of time called "Early," "Middle," and "Late." Then it is divided again into even smaller time-chunks with formal names like "Oxfordian," as well as ten others. Fifty-six million years is a long time, and no dinosaur lived for the entire Jurassic period.

Fossils are the remains of living things preserved in stone that was once mud or sand. Dinosaur fossils are only found in specific layers of rock that were deposited as sand and dirt during a small part of the Jurassic. These remains help us learn about what lived during the Jurassic.

Some of the most famous dinosaurs lived during the Late Jurassic. Fossils of the spike-tailed Stegosaurus and the fearsome birdlike Allosaurus are found together in western North America, along with the giant dino-cousins, Apatosaurus and Brontosaurus. Not all dinosaurs lived at the same time or even in the same place. The oldest dinosaurs of the Early Jurassic are remarkable, like the ancestor of Stegosaurus, the armor-studded Scelidosaurus from England.

The first Jurassic dinosaur fossils found were named Megalosaurus in 1824. They were from Middle Jurassic age rocks in England. Megalosaurus fossils helped define what it means to be a dinosaur. Middle Jurassic fossils remain elusive to this day. In fact, modern paleontologists are still discovering new animals and plants from extinct streams and ponds that once offered Jurassic dinosaurs a drink.

As you read this book, think about each dinosaur and what its life might have been like. Take a trip to your library and read as many dinosaur books as you can find. Visit your local museum and learn more about the dinosaurs that might have lived in your own backyard.

Introduction

Come along with us on a journey deep into the earth's history, to a time long before the first humans ever existed. A time when giants roamed the earth and reptiles ruled the skies. A time of absolute beauty and extreme danger—this is the Late Jurassic.

We are now about 150 million years away from the earth as we know it. Standing in lush green surroundings, you take a deep breath and notice how thick the air is with humidity. The unique smell of wet and decomposing plant matter overwhelms you as the sound of insects rings endlessly in your ears. The air is stifling hot, making it exhausting to get around. The Late Jurassic does not welcome visitors.

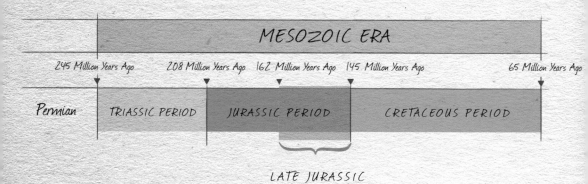

MESOZOIC ERA

245 Million Years Ago · 208 Million Years Ago · 162 Million Years Ago · 145 Million Years Ago · 65 Million Years Ago

Permian · TRIASSIC PERIOD · JURASSIC PERIOD · CRETACEOUS PERIOD

LATE JURASSIC

The Jurassic period is the middle portion of the Mesozoic era, better known as "the age of reptiles." During the latter part of this period, the earth is experiencing significant changes, including volcanic activity due to shifting tectonic plates. The once supercontinent, Pangaea, is now divided into four landmasses consisting of South America and Africa, Western Europe and Asia, Australia and Antarctica, and North America.

The eruptions from volcanoes along with greenhouse gasses are raising temperatures worldwide, several degrees warmer than in modern times. Because of this, there are no polar ice caps, leading to extremely high sea levels. The two largest bodies of water, the Pacific Ocean and the Tethys Ocean, take up 80 percent of the earth's surface, while the Atlantic Ocean is just beginning to appear as a small inland sea. The world is a warm, wet, and tropical place—the perfect environment for plant and animal development.

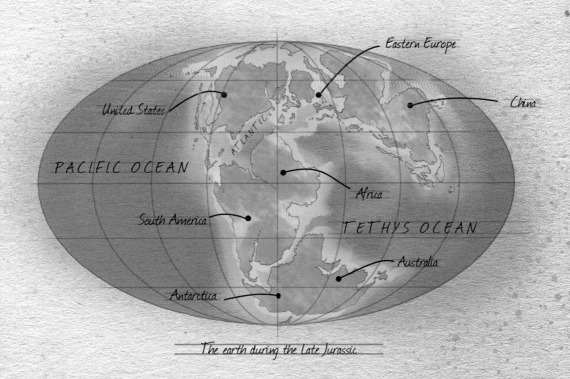

The earth during the Late Jurassic

Around you the landscape is composed of tall conifer trees like the Araucaria (see fig. a) and Ginkgo trees. Low lying club mosses (see fig. b) and Neocalamites, or horsetail plants (see fig. c), stem from and around freshwater ponds and creeks. Ferns and cycads, like Otozamites (see fig. d), dominate as ground cover and low trees. Everywhere you look you are surrounded by greenery. This greenery fuels the growth of enormous plant-eating dinosaurs.

Some dinosaur species are rapidly evolving larger in a race to outgrow the predators that feed on them, some reaching lengths of over 100 feet. As groups of dinosaurs, such as the sauropods, evolve into larger species, so do their predators. Animals like Allosaurus and Torvosaurus are becoming apex predators reaching over 30 feet in length, armed with weaponry designed to dispatch their prey quickly and efficiently. While some herbivorous dinosaurs are finding safety in size, others are beginning to develop armor or speed as a way to elude the jaws of predators.

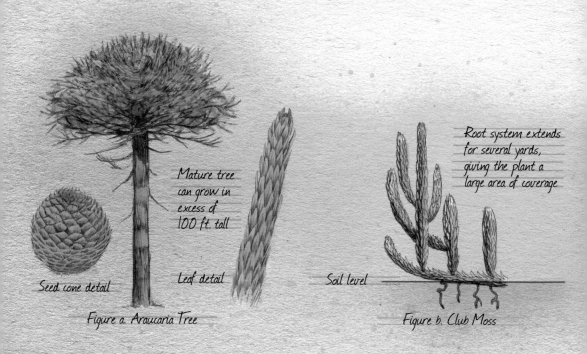

Mature tree can grow in excess of 100 ft. tall

Seed cone detail

Leaf detail

Figure a. Araucaria Tree

Root system extends for several yards, giving the plant a large area of coverage

Soil level

Figure b. Club Moss

Danger comes in all sizes, as smaller predators are filling evolutionary niches and becoming specialized hunters. Gliding through the air from trees is becoming a new means of hunting for the smaller theropod dinosaurs. This method will soon give rise to the first true birds. But for now, pterosaurs, or "flying reptiles," are the undisputed rulers of the sky. Though diminutive in size, their adaptations and ability for flight are unmatched by any other vertebrates.

Continue along on our journey as we dive deeper into the wildlife of the Late Jurassic than ever before, coming face to face with everything from early mammals to super predators. In this book, you will discover how some dinosaurs developed techniques for hunting while others used new adaptations for self-defense. Page by page, you'll see a first-hand, intimate account of what it was like to stand ankle-high next to the largest group of animals to walk the earth. These animals towered over our closest relatives—the early mammals—as they began to stake their claim in a world dominated by dinosaurs. This is the Late Jurassic as never seen before.

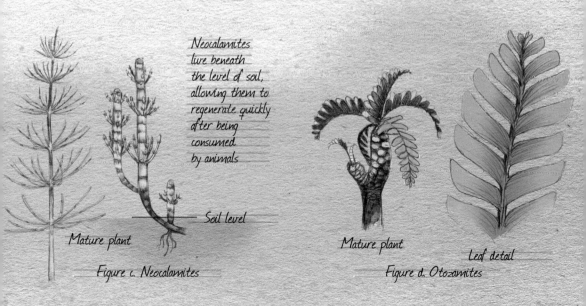

Neocalamites live beneath the level of soil, allowing them to regenerate quickly after being consumed by animals

Soil level

Mature plant

Figure c. Neocalamites

Mature plant

Leaf detail

Figure d. Otozamites

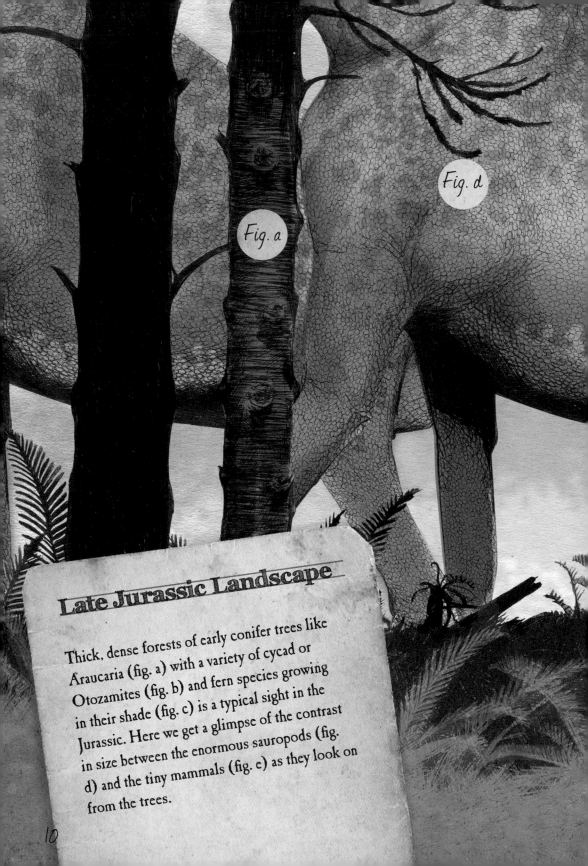

Fig. a

Fig. d

Late Jurassic Landscape

Thick, dense forests of early conifer trees like Araucaria (fig. a) with a variety of cycad or Otozamites (fig. b) and fern species growing in their shade (fig. c) is a typical sight in the Jurassic. Here we get a glimpse of the contrast in size between the enormous sauropods (fig. d) and the tiny mammals (fig. e) as they look on from the trees.

The Theropods

Our journey begins in search of the largest predators to ever walk the earth: the theropods. You find yourself standing on a vast flood plain. The ground is dry, but in a few months, during the rainy season, this area will be submerged underwater. For now, it serves as an open path for both predators and prey to travel freely. Beneath you lies a mosaic of footprints, including small and large three-toed impressions. The largest of these footprints is 1.5 feet from toe to heel. This, without a doubt, belongs to a large theropod. It is freshly made.

The cold feeling of fear runs through you as you realize the dinosaur could be anywhere. Without thinking twice, you begin to run for cover toward the nearest cluster of trees. You can feel its presence behind you, but cannot force yourself to turn around. Within the relative safety of the trees, you keep running toward the densest part of the woods, where you hope it cannot follow you. From the shelter of a thick trunk, you slowly turn to see your pursuer.

9 feet

6 feet

3 feet

Standing around 10 feet tall, with its head hung low to avoid detection, the theropod gradually cocks its head to one side to get a better look at you. It raises its snout and sniffs the air. The look in its eye, one of focus and determination, reminds you of a bird of prey. There is no question: You are being hunted. With small horns above its eyes and dagger-sized, hooked claws hanging from its thick arms, this animal instills the kind of fear no other living animal can. You can feel your heartbeat through your chest as it cautiously steps closer and again sniffs the air. It doesn't recognize your scent, and it doesn't know what to make of you. With a loud snort, it turns its back and calmly walks away as its long tail follows. You have just survived an encounter with a Late Jurassic theropod.

In 1841, when Sir Richard Owen coined the term *dinosaur*, meaning "terrible lizard," he must have had theropods in mind. Theropods were a group of dinosaurs that included some of the largest and most fearsome carnivorous animals to ever exist. Though some were truly scary, in reality, many were no larger than a turkey.

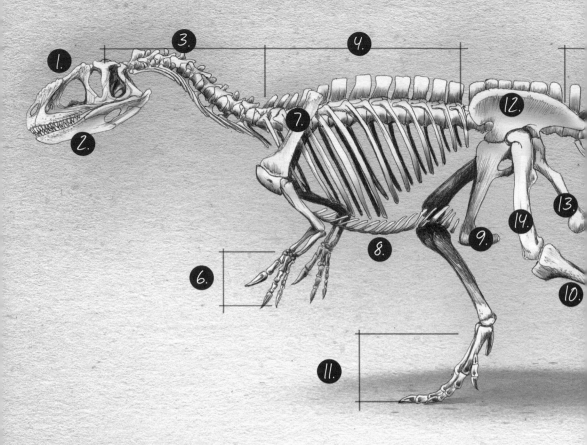

Theropods were a very diverse group of animals known for being bipedal, meaning they used two legs for walking, and most were known for being carnivorous. Some theropods developed instincts for caring for their young and finding mates, much like birds do today. As a matter of fact, theropod dinosaurs have not technically become extinct, as some evolved into modern birds.

Theropods of the Late Jurassic

By the Late Jurassic, several species of theropods had reached unprecedented size. This trend called "gigantism" was only the beginning. Soon super predators reaching 40 to 55 feet in length began to dominate the earth in the following period: the Cretaceous. But in the Jurassic, 30- to 35-foot-long theropods were at the top of the food chain. Many of them had hands built like the talons of an eagle, with a razor-sharp thumb claw over 9 inches long. Because prey animals were becoming larger, some theropods may have developed hunting techniques such as pack hunting, where several individuals worked together to bring down larger prey.

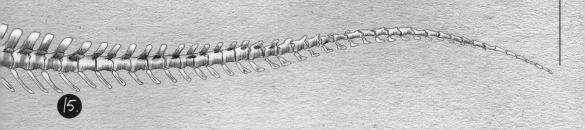

15

Anatomy of a Late Jurassic theropod skeleton

1. skull	6. manus	11. pes
2. mandible	7. scapula	12. ilium
3. cervical vertebrae	8. gastralia	13. ischium
4. dorsal vertebrae	9. pubis	14. femur
5. caudal vertebrae	10. tibia and fibula	15. chevrons

The smaller theropods were making their mark as well. Species like Archaeopteryx lithographica and Yi qi developed an ingenious method of hunting for food. By gliding down from trees, they captured prey unreachable by any other means, as well as evaded predators. They were the first airborne dinosaurs. Later as these species evolved to become skilled fliers, they led the way to the first true birds. Other species like Ornitholestes hermanni and Guanlong wucaii were carving out a place of their own between both giant and small hunters. Swift and agile, they were proficient at running down prey generally too large for the small theropods, as well as the smaller theropods themselves.

The following pages will bring you closer to the Late Jurassic theropods as you examine the hunting techniques and adaptations developed through millions of years of evolution.

Allosaurus fragilis

Location Observed: *Colorado and Utah, United States*

Family: *Allosauridae*

Length: *30 feet (9 meters)*

Height: *9.5 feet (3 meters)*

Weight: *1.7 tons*

Temperament: *Aggressive*

Coarse, scaly skin

Long, curved neck

Powerful arms with three claws for grasping prey

Narrow, slender built body

Long, strong legs

9 feet

6 feet

3 feet

Allosaurus is one of the largest predators of the Late Jurassic

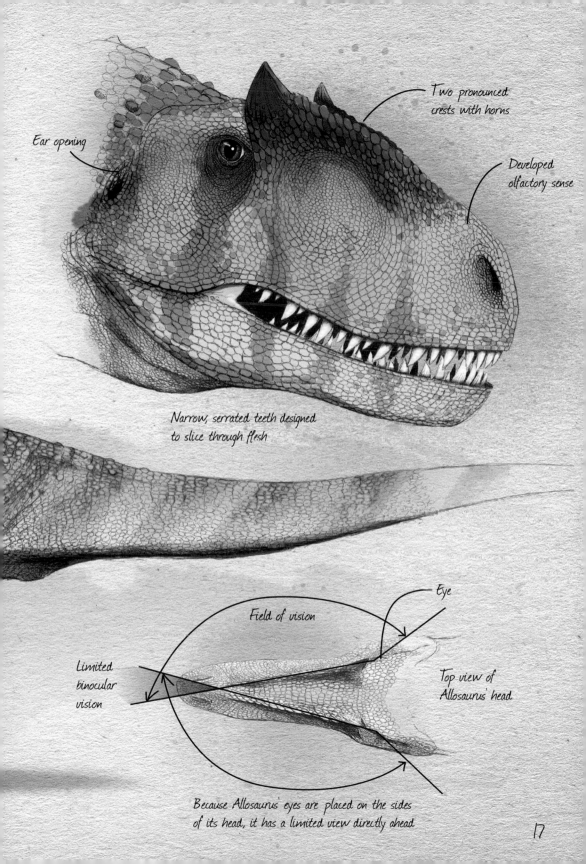

Two pronounced
crests with horns

Ear opening

Developed
olfactory sense

Narrow, serrated teeth designed
to slice through flesh

Eye

Field of vision

Limited
binocular
vision

Top view of
Allosaurus' head

Because Allosaurus' eyes are placed on the sides
of its head, it has a limited view directly ahead

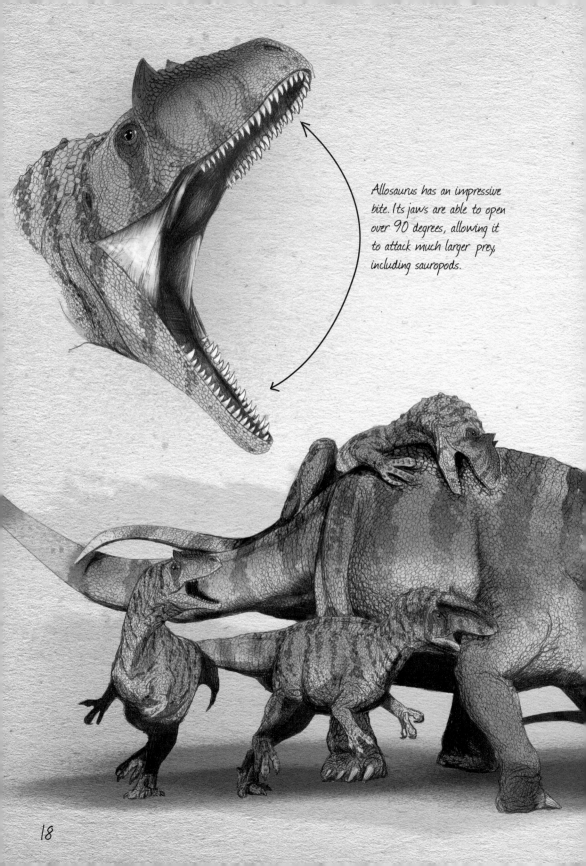

Allosaurus has an impressive
bite. Its jaws are able to open
over 90 degrees, allowing it
to attack much larger prey,
including sauropods.

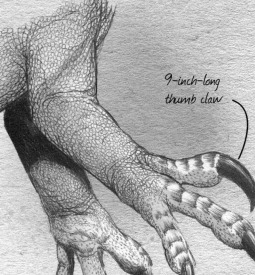

Equally as dangerous as its bite, Allosaurus' forelimbs contain enormous claws used to dispatch prey or act as meat hooks to seize larger animals

9-inch-long thumb claw

A young sauropod falls prey to a pack of Allosaurs. Using its flexible jaws and grasping claws, Allosaurus slows down and eventually brings the sauropod's neck closer to the ground where it can be killed.

Archaeopteryx lithographica

Location Observed: Southern Germany

Family: Archaeopterygidae

Length: 1.7 feet (.5 meter)

Height: 2.3 feet (.7 meter) wingspan

Weight: 1.1 pounds

Temperament: Cautious, curious

Long feathers create shape of tail

Archaeopteryx tail detail
(Top view)

Covered in dark feathers

Long, slim neck

Three individual digits
with claws

Three-clawed wings

Archaeopteryx wing detail

Feathers anchored to forearm
and second digit

Killing claw on second digit

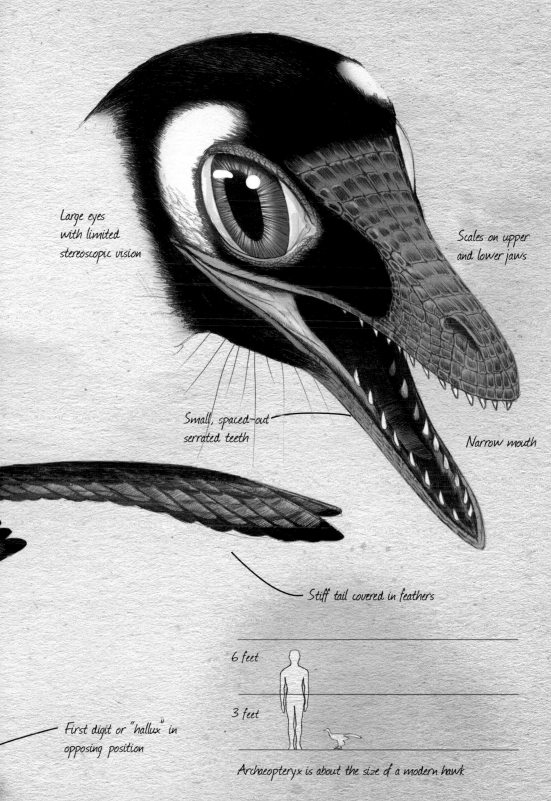

Large eyes
with limited
stereoscopic vision

Scales on upper
and lower jaws

Small, spaced-out
serrated teeth

Narrow mouth

Stiff tail covered in feathers

6 feet

3 feet

First digit or "hallux" in
opposing position

Archaeopteryx is about the size of a modern hawk

Ceratosaurus nasicornis

Location Observed: *Colorado and Utah, United States*

Family: *Ceratosauridae*

Length: *20 feet (6 meters)*

Height: *7 feet (2 meters)*

Weight: *1,300 pounds*

Temperament: *Extremely aggressive*

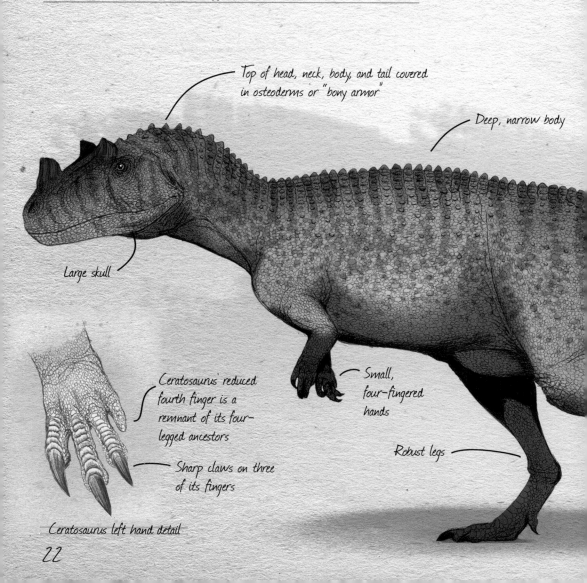

Top of head, neck, body, and tail covered in osteoderms or "bony armor"

Deep, narrow body

Large skull

Ceratosaurus' reduced fourth finger is a remnant of its four-legged ancestors

Small, four-fingered hands

Sharp claws on three of its fingers

Robust legs

Ceratosaurus left hand detail

Three large horns used as mating display

Small eyes

Very large, flattened teeth

Lightly built jaw

Very deep and narrow tail

6 feet

3 feet

At 20 feet long, Ceratosaurus is considered a medium-sized theropod

23

Compsognathus longipes

Location Observed: Southern Germany and Southern France

Family: Compsognathidae

Length: 4 feet (1.25 meters)

Height: 1 foot (.4 meter)

Weight: 5.5 pounds

Temperament: Shy, elusive

Using its small serrated teeth and flexible hands, Compsognathus quickly devours a small water snake

Long, narrow build

Three-clawed forelimbs

Compsognathus hand detail

Very long, thin legs designed for speed

Relatively large feet

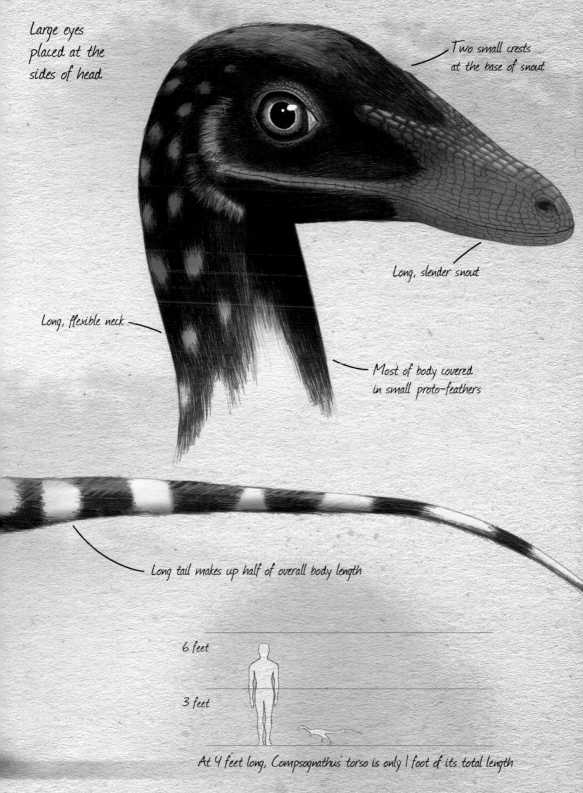

Large eyes
placed at the
sides of head

Two small crests
at the base of snout

Long, slender snout

Long, flexible neck

Most of body covered
in small proto-feathers

Long tail makes up half of overall body length

6 feet

3 feet

At 4 feet long, Compsognathus' torso is only 1 foot of its total length

Guanlong wucaii

Location Observed: *Xinjiang, China*

Family: *Proceratosauridae*

Length: *11 feet (3.5 meters)*

Height: *5 feet (1.5 meters)*

Weight: *250 pounds*

Temperament: *Aggressive, territorial*

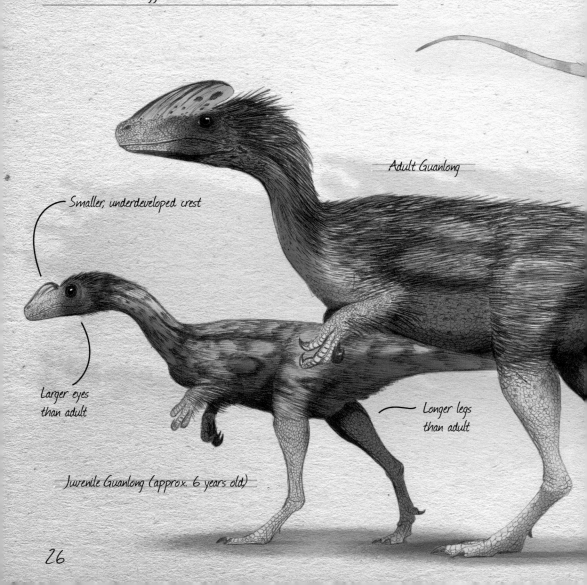

Adult Guanlong

Smaller, underdeveloped crest

Larger eyes than adult

Longer legs than adult

Juvenile Guanlong (approx. 6 years old)

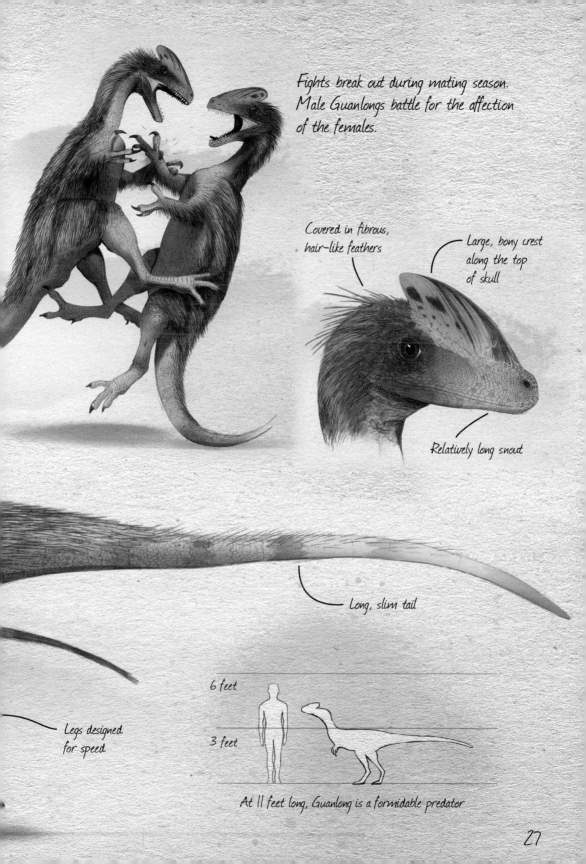

Fights break out during mating season. Male Guanlongs battle for the affection of the females.

Covered in fibrous, hair-like feathers

Large, bony crest along the top of skull

Relatively long snout

Long, slim tail

Legs designed for speed

6 feet

3 feet

At 11 feet long, Guanlong is a formidable predator

Ornitholestes hermanni

Location Observed: Wyoming, United States

Family: Coeluridae

Length: 7 feet (2 meters)

Height: 2 feet (.6 meter)

Weight: 30 pounds

Temperament: Aggressive

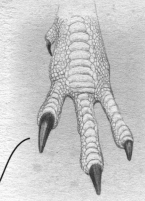

Second toe is shorter,
with a longer claw

Ornitholestes left foot detail

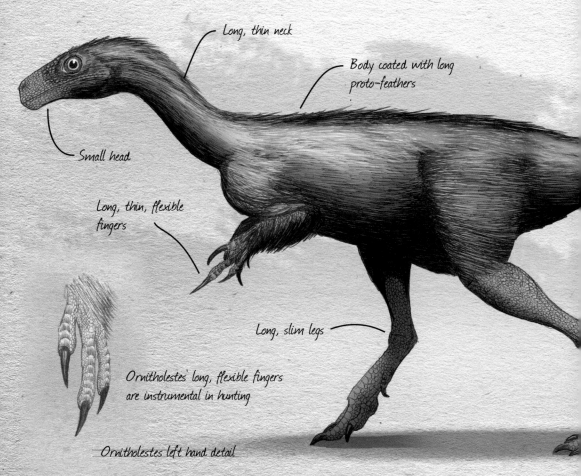

Long, thin neck

Body coated with long
proto-feathers

Small head

Long, thin, flexible
fingers

Ornitholestes' long, flexible fingers
are instrumental in hunting

Long, slim legs

Ornitholestes left hand detail

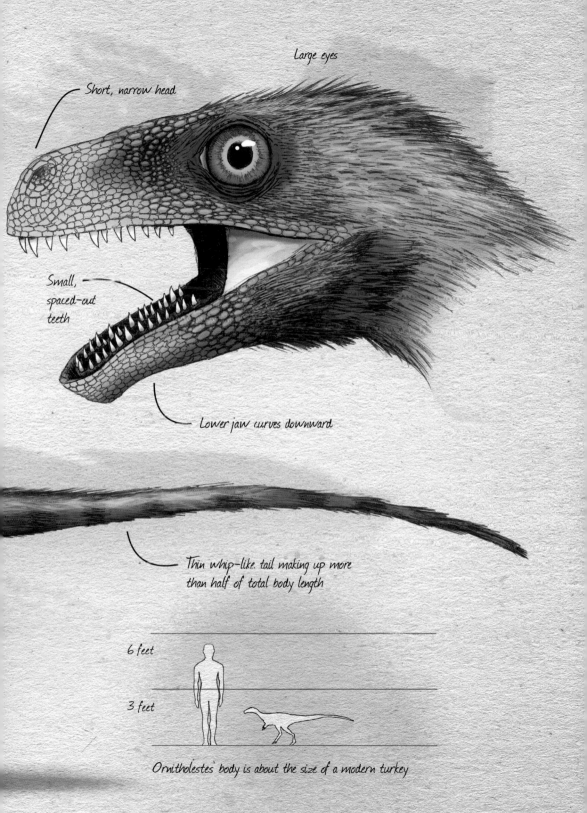

Large eyes

Short, narrow head

Small,
spaced-out
teeth

Lower jaw curves downward

Thin whip-like tail making up more
than half of total body length

6 feet

3 feet

Ornitholestes' body is about the size of a modern turkey

Torvosaurus tanneri

Location Observed: *Colorado, Wyoming, and Utah, United States*

Family: *Megalosauridae*

Length: *33 feet (10 meters)*

Height: *9 feet (3 meters)*

Weight: *2 tons*

Temperament: *Extremely aggressive*

Dermal spines on head and neck

Long body

Large head

Powerful arms
with large
thumb claw

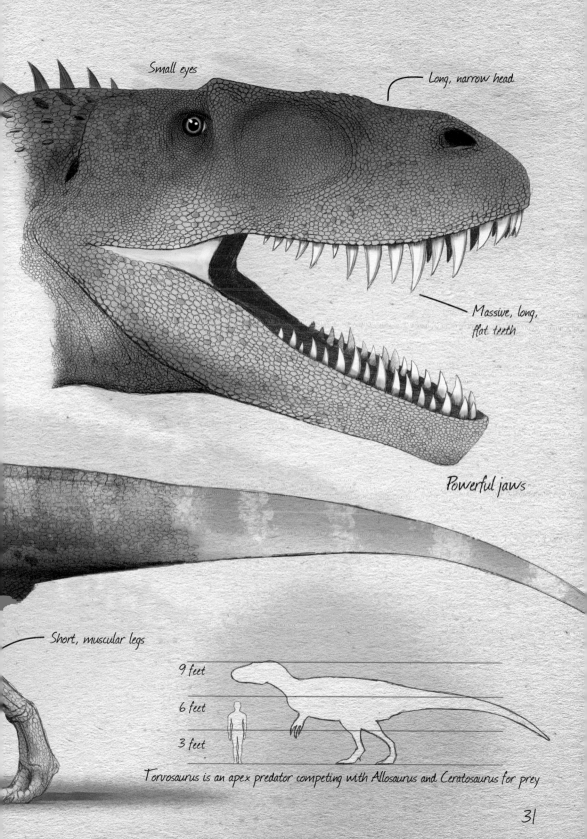

Small eyes

Long, narrow head

Massive, long,
flat teeth

Powerful jaws

Short, muscular legs

9 feet

6 feet

3 feet

Torvosaurus is an apex predator competing with Allosaurus and Ceratosaurus for prey

Thick, muscular neck used to pull large pieces of meat from prey

From the front, Torvosaurus presents a broad profile to intimidate animals challenging it for food

Large feet

With teeth reaching 5 inches (9 inches including the root), Torvosaurus is able to take down prey much larger than itself

Detail of serrations

Front view

Side view

Torvosaurus tooth detail

Teeth are equipped with fine serrations on the front and back, which act like a saw that cuts through meat

Both a predator and scavenger, Torvosaurus' size allows it to take over another dinosaur's meal

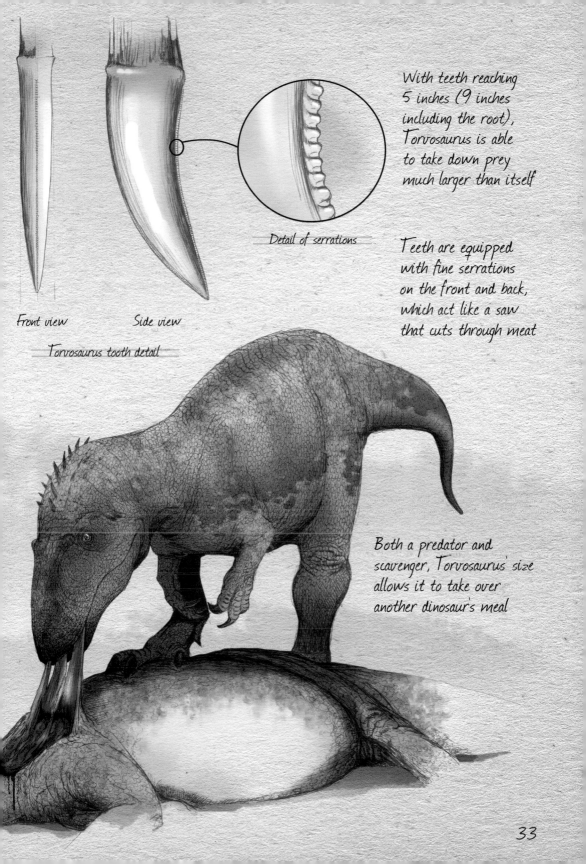

Yangchuanosaurus shangyouensis

Location Observed: Yongchuan, China

Family: Metriacanthosauridae

Length: 35 feet (11 meters)

Height: 10 feet (3 meters)

Weight: 3 tons

Temperament: Extremely aggressive

Long, curved neck

Tall ridge along back

Deep, narrow torso

Strong arms with three gripping claws

Long legs designed for running

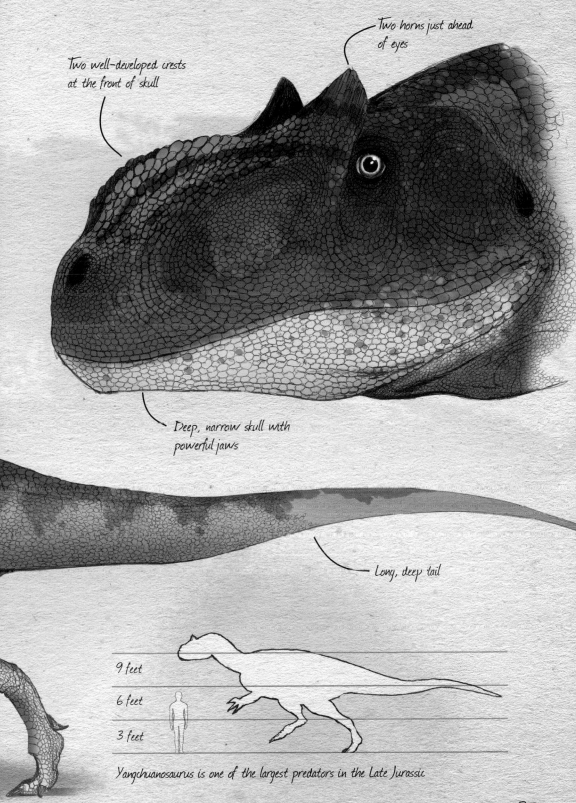

Two horns just ahead of eyes

Two well-developed crests at the front of skull

Deep, narrow skull with powerful jaws

Long, deep tail

9 feet

6 feet

3 feet

Yangchuanosaurus is one of the largest predators in the Late Jurassic

As one of the largest predators in the Late
Jurassic, Yangchuanosaurus hunted large game

A pack of adult Yangchuanosaurus attack a
Mamenchisaurus using their claws and powerful
bites to bring it closer to the ground where they
can kill it

Mamenchisaurus is an Asian sauropod reaching lengths of up to 115 feet and weighing up to 75 tons. It is known for having the longest neck of all sauropods.

Yi qi

Location Observed: Hebei, China

Family: Scansoriopterygidae

Length: 12 inches (.3 meter)

Height: 18 inches (.45 meter) wingspan

Weight: .84 pound

Temperament: Shy, elusive

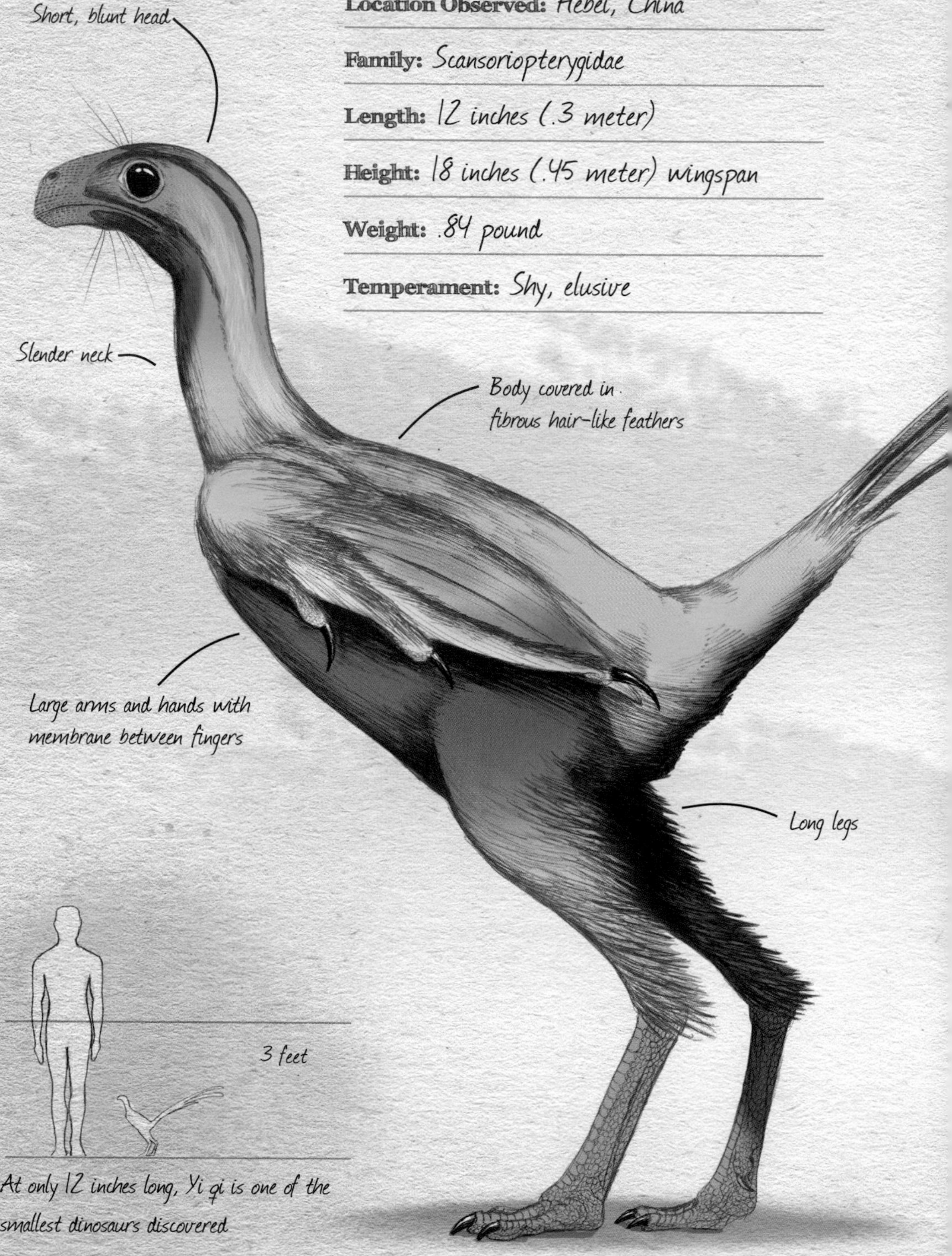

Short, blunt head

Slender neck

Body covered in fibrous hair-like feathers

Large arms and hands with membrane between fingers

Long legs

3 feet

At only 12 inches long, Yi qi is one of the smallest dinosaurs discovered

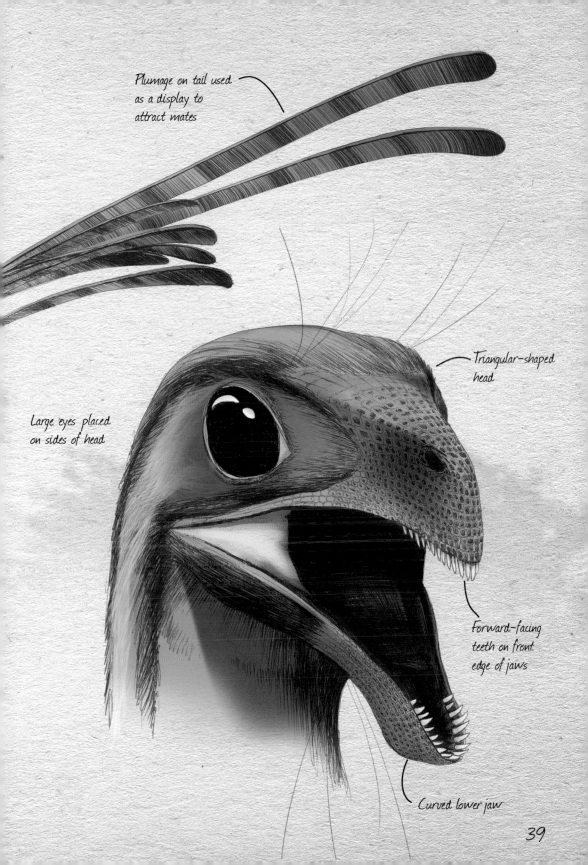

Plumage on tail used
as a display to
attract mates

Triangular-shaped
head

Large eyes placed
on sides of head

Forward-facing
teeth on front
edge of jaws

Curved lower jaw

From tree-borne to airborne, Yi qi takes flight

1. Yi qi is adept at climbing
   trees by using its hands,
   claws, and long arms

2. Once it sees prey, it opens
   its arms and extends the
   membrane to form wings

Long claws used for climbing

Bone extending from wrist spreads
membrane to create larger wing surface.
When arm is contracted, the bone folds
back along forearm.

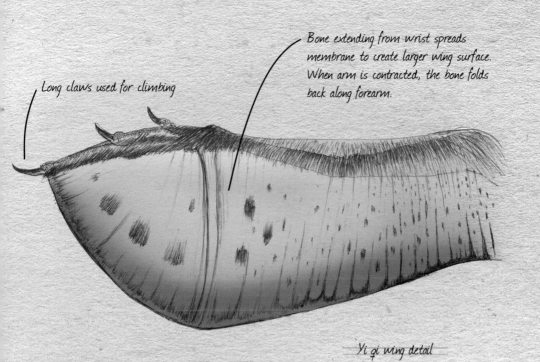

Yi qi wing detail

3. Pushing off the tree with its long legs
   like a catapult, Yi qi takes flight, gliding
   towards its prey before landing on the
   ground or on another tree

The Mammals

It's another typical day in the Late Jurassic, hot and steamy with the constant harassment of biting insects. You escape into the shade of a grove to avoid the sun, and you are surprised to see the trees alive with movement. Jumping from branch to branch, there are several small animals with long tails interacting playfully. They look like a mixture of a squirrel and an opossum and act very much like modern-day mammals. They have total command of the trees where they feel at home, oblivious to any of the dangers that come with living on the ground. These animals are a startling contrast to the other wildlife experienced in the Jurassic. Watching them almost makes you forget you are 150 million years away from the earth you know. These are the early mammals, your great ancestors, and a glimpse of what evolution has in store for the earth.

The first true mammals began to appear around the Late Triassic period, about 50 to 75 million years before the Late Jurassic. They evolved alongside the dinosaurs, but remained small, carving out evolutionary niches and not competing directly with them. Their small size was a blessing in disguise, as it allowed them to survive

past the extinction event that killed off the dinosaurs around 65 million years ago. Afterwards, the mammals would flourish and slowly begin to evolve into larger species, giving rise to early primates and ultimately humans.

Mammals of the Late Jurassic

By the Late Jurassic, mammals adapted to different lifestyles, including species like Fruitafossor windscheffeli, who developed specialized traits designed for digging and eating termites and ants. Others like Castorocauda lutrasimilis made the water their home by evolving the attributes necessary for a semi-aquatic life, one similar to a modern-day otter.

In this section, we will take a look at two well-documented species: Shenshou lui, an arboreal or "tree-dwelling" animal from China, and Juramaia sinensis, whose name means "Jurassic Mother," also from China. Shenshou evolved hands and feet with opposable fingers perfect for grasping branches and a prehensile tail capable of gripping onto trees and acting like a fifth limb. Juramaia is equally at home in the trees as on the ground and is built more like a small mouse or shrew. What makes Juramaia more notable is that it is considered to be the first placental mammal, meaning it gave birth to live young which developed in a womb. These are two of the early mammals who lived among dinosaurs and foreshadow the evolutionary changes the earth is soon to experience.

Shenshou lui

Location Observed: Liaoning, China

Family: Mammalia

Length: 1 foot (.3 meter)

Weight: 10 ounces

Temperament: Cautious

Large eyes allow Shenshou to see in low-light conditions

Very large incisors

6 feet

3 feet

Shenshou is about the size of a squirrel

Shenshou live almost exclusively in trees and are omnivorous, eating insects, nuts, and fruit

Shenshou's hands show a thumb adapted for grasping branches

Long, prehensile tail

Juramaia sinensis

Location Observed: Liaoning, China

Family: Mammalia

Length: 5 inches (.12 meter)

Weight: 15 grams

Temperament: Reclusive, shy

Long tail covered in hair

Feet designed for both climbing and running on the ground

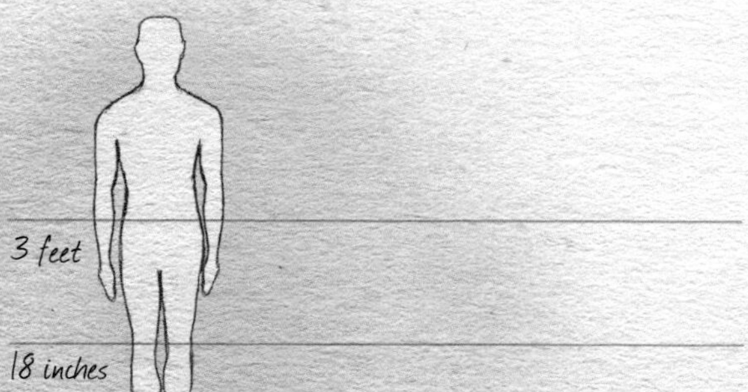

3 feet

18 inches

Juramaia is about the size of a shrew

Long, conical teeth
used for catching and eating
insects and worms

Body covered in
short hair

Long snout

Juramaia head detail

47

Pronunciation Key

Theropods (Theer-uh-pods)
Allosaurus fragilis (Al-oh-sore-us, fraj-ill-iss)
Archaeopteryx lithographica (Are-key-op-trex, lith-o-graf-e-ka)
Ceratosaurus nasicornis (Sir-at-toe-sore-us, nay-si-corn-iss)
Compsognathus longipes (Comp-sog-nay-thus, long-gipes)
Guanlong wucaii (Ga-wan-long, goo-kai)
Ornitholestes hermanni (Or-nith-oh-less-teaze, her-man-knee)
Torvosaurus tanneri (Tor-vo-sore-us, tan-nery)
Yangchuanosaurus shangyouensis (Yan-chwahn-oh-sore-us, shang-u-en-sis)
Yi qi (Ee-chee)

Mammals
Shenshou lui (Shen-shoe, le-oh)
Juramaia sinensis (Joor-ah-my-ah, sin-n-sis)

About the Authors

Juan Carlos Alonso
Juan Carlos Alonso (author and illustrator) is a Cuban American graphic designer, creative director, and illustrator. He has over 30 years experience in the graphic design/illustration field. In 1992 he founded Alonso & Company, a creative boutique specializing in branding, design, and advertising. His passion for nature has taken him around the world, from Australia to the Galapagos Islands, to study animals. Along with his work in the graphic arts, he is also an accomplished wildlife sculptor, focusing mostly on prehistoric animals.

Gregory S. Paul
Gregory S. Paul (co-author) is an American freelance researcher, author, and illustrator who works in paleontology. He is best known for his work and research on theropod dinosaurs and his detailed illustrations, both live and skeletal. Professionally investigating and restoring dinosaurs for three decades, Paul received an on-screen credit as a dinosaur specialist on *Jurassic Park* and Discovery Channel's *When Dinosaurs Roamed America* and *Dinosaur Planet*. He is the author and illustrator of *Predatory Dinosaurs of the World* (1988), *The Complete Illustrated Guide to Dinosaur Skeletons* (1996), *Dinosaurs of the Air* (2001), *The Princeton Field Guide To Dinosaurs* (2010), *Gregory S. Paul's Dinosaur Coffee Table Book* (2010), and editor of *The Scientific American Book of Dinosaurs* (2000). Paul has named over twelve prehistoric animal species and has had two dinosaur species named after him (*Cryptovolans pauli* and *Sellacoxa pauli*) based on his innovative theories.